North American Indians Today

North American Indians Today

Apache

Cherokee

Cheyenne

Comanche

Creek

Crow

Huron

Iroquois

Navajo

Ojibwa

Osage

Potawatomi

Pueblo

Seminole

Sioux

North American
Indians Today

Iroquois

by
Kenneth McIntosh
and
Marsha McIntosh

Mason Crest Publishers

Philadelphia

The authors wish to thank the people who helped with this book: Brian Patterson, Birdy Burdeck, Kay Olan, Jessica Howard, Mark Emery, and Mike Tarbell.

Mason Crest Publishers Inc.
370 Reed Road
Broomall, Pennsylvania 19008
(866) MCP-BOOK (toll free)

First printing
1 2 3 4 5 6 7 8 9 10
Library of Congress Cataloging-in-Publication Data on file at the Library of Congress.
ISBN: 1-59084-671-0
1-59084-663-X (series)

Design by Lori Holland.
Composition by Bytheway Publishing Services, Binghamton, New York.
Cover design by Benjamin Stewart.
Printed and bound in the Hashemite Kingdom of Jordan.

Photography by Benjamin Stewart. Pictures on pp. 37, 63, 87 courtesy of Turning Stone Casino; p. 48 courtesy of Jonathan Maracle; pp. 57, 60, 74 courtesy of the Oneida Nation; p. 77 courtesy of John Patterson; p. 78 courtesy of Joanne Shenandoah; p. 79 courtesy of Graham Greene; p. 80 courtesy of Tom Porter; p. 84 courtesy of Viola Ruelke Gommer; p. 86 courtesy of the National Museum of the American Indian. Picture on p. 6 by Keith Rosco.

Contents

Why is it so important that Indians be brought into the "mainstream" of American life?
I would not know how to interpret this phrase to my people.
The closest I would be able to come would be "a big wide river".
Am I then to tell my people that they are to be thrown into the big, wide river of the United States?

Earl Old Person
Blackfeet Tribal Chairman

Introduction

In the midst of twenty-first-century North America, how do the very first North Americans hold on to their unique cultural identity? At the same time, how do they adjust to the real demands of the modern world? Earl Old Person's quote on the opposite page expresses the difficulty of achieving this balance. Even the common values of the rest of North America—like fitting into the "mainstream"—may seem strange or undesireable to North American Indians. How can these groups of people thrive and prosper in the twenty-first century without losing their traditions, the ways of thinking and living that have been handed down to them by their ancestors? How can they keep from drowning in North America's "big, wide river"?

Thoughts from the Series Consultant

Each of the books in this series was written with the help of Native scholars and tribal leaders from the particular tribe. Based on oral histories as well as written documents, these books describe the current strategies of each Native nation to develop its economy while maintaining strong ties with its culture. As a result, you may find that these books read far differently from other books about Native Americans.

Over the past centuries, Native groups have faced increasing pressure to conform to the wishes of the governments that took their lands. Often brutally inhumane methods were implemented to change Native social systems. These books describe the ways that Native groups refused to be passive recipients of change, even in the face of these past atrocities. Heroic individuals worked to fit external changes into local conditions. This struggle continues today.

The legacy of the past still haunts the psyche of both Native and non-Native people of North America; hopefully, these books will help correct some misunderstandings. And even with the difficulties encountered by past and current Native leaders, Native nations continue to thrive. As this series illustrates, Native populations continue to increase—and they have clearly persevered against incredible odds. North American culture's big, wide river may be deep and cold—but Native Americans are good swimmers!

—Martha McCollough

Breaking Stereotypes

One way that some North Americans may "drown" Native culture is by using stereotypes to think about North American Indians. When we use stereotypes to think about a group of people, we assume things about them because of their race or cultural group. Instead of taking time to understand individual differences and situations, we lump together everyone in a certain group. In reality, though, every person is different. More than two million Native people live in North America, and they are as *diverse* as any other group. Each one is unique.

Even if we try hard to avoid stereotypes, however, it isn't always easy to know what words to use. Should we call the people who are native to North America Native Americans—or American Indians—or just Indians?

The word "Indian" probably comes from a mistake—when Christopher Columbus arrived in the New World, he thought he had reached India, so he called the people he found there Indians. Some people feel it doesn't make much sense to call Native Americans "Indians." (Suppose Columbus had thought he landed in China instead of India; would we today call Native people "Chinese"?) Other scholars disagree; for example, Russell Means, Native politician and activist, claims that the word "Indian" comes from Columbus saying the native people were *en Dios*—"in God," or naturally spiritual.

Many Canadians use the term "First Nations" to refer to the Native peoples who live there, and people in the United States usually speak of Native Americans. Most Native people we talked to while we were writing these books prefer the simple term "Indian"—or they would rather use the names of their tribes. (We have used the term "North American Indians" for our series to distinguish this group of people from the inhabitants of India.)

Even the definition of what makes a person "Indian" varies. The U.S. government recognizes certain groups as tribal nations (almost 500 in all). Each nation then decides how it will enroll people as members of that tribe. Tribes may require a particular amount of Indian blood, tribal membership of the father or the mother, or other *criteria*. Some enrolled tribal members who are legally "Indian" may not look Native at all; many have blond hair and blue eyes and others have clearly African features. At the same time, there are thousands of Native people whose tribes have not yet been officially recognized by the government.

We have done our best to write books that are as free from stereotypes as possible. But you as the reader also play a part. After reading one of these books, we hope you won't think: "The Cheyenne are all like this" or "Iroquois are all like that." Each person in this world is unique, whatever their culture. Stereotypes shut people's minds—but these books are intended to open your mind. North American Indians today have much wisdom and beauty to offer.

Some people consider American Indians to be a historical topic only, but Indians today are living, contributing members of North American society. The contributions of the various Indian cultures enrich our world—and North America would be a very different place without the Native people who live there. May they never be lost in North America's "big, wide river"!

This painting, titled Creation, *by Pauline Lahache, a Mohawk from Kahnawake, shows the Great Turtle rising from the water that covered the world at the time Sky Woman fell.*

Chapter 1

Creation

"Se: ko ska: ne: go: wa."
("May a great peace be within you," in the Oneida language.)

Many people have seen and visited the UN building in New York City. They know the United Nations was created in 1945 in an attempt to unite the nations of the world for peace. But most people don't know there is another set of "united nations" in upstate New York—or that this original united nations has lasted for almost 900 years!

The Haudenosaunee are a confederation of Indian nations united to keep peace and achieve common goals. *Haudenosaunee* means "People of the Longhouse." It is pronounced ho-deh-no-sho-nee—and "Longhouse" refers to the buildings they lived in long ago and also to the religious and political ways they continue to follow. They are often called the Iroquois (pronounced ear-uh-kwa). That name comes from their old enemies, the Wyandotte. Iroquois means "snakes," referring to the way they would sneak up on their enemies in battle.

Today there are more than 74,000 Haudenosaunee; most of them live in the northeastern United States and southeastern Canada. They belong to six "nations":

1. Seneca or *Onondowahgah*, "the People of the Great Hill."
2. Cayuga or *Guyohkohnyoh*, "the People of the Great Swamp."
3. Onondaga or *Onundagaono*, "the People of the Hills."
4. Oneida or *Onayotekaono*, "the People of the Upright Stone."
5. Mohawk or *Kanienka:haka*, "the People of the Flint" or "People of the Place of Crystals."
6. Tuscarora or *Ska-Ruh-Reh*, "the People Who Wear Shirts."

The Haudenosaunee have ancient sacred oral traditions that explain life's meaning for them. These could be compared to the Jewish or Christian Bible, except they were passed down through the centuries by living people's voices rather than in books. Details of these oral traditions vary between the six nations, but the main events are similar.

Corn is one of the "Three Sisters," the plants that came up after the burial of Sky Woman's daughter, Mother Earth. Corn, beans, and squash were traditionally staple crops for the Haudenosaunee.

> If you read the first chapters of Genesis (the first book in the Jewish and Christian scripture), you will find parallels between the creation story found there and that of the Haudenosaunee. The importance of a tree, the role of the first woman, and the battle between good and evil are interesting areas of similarity.

A contemporary Iroquois storyteller might tell a sacred story that would sound like this:

Now I will tell you how everything began. Before this world in which we live, there was another world—the sky world. The sky world was not un-like our own: beings lived there like ourselves—two-legged, four-legged, and winged beings. Everyone lived peacefully in the sky world. Many sorts of trees grew up there, but one tree was very special. It grew in the very center of the above world, and it gave light to the entire world, since the sun had not been created yet. This sacred tree was not supposed to be plucked or disturbed by any being in the above world. It was the source of peace and health that everyone in that world experienced.

One man was the caretaker of the sacred tree. He married, and not long after, his wife became pregnant. She was very bossy and demanding; the husband tried to make her happy, but she was never pleased with his ef-forts. As women do when they are with child, the woman craved all sorts of different foods. She became very curious about the unusual fruits that grew on the special tree.

Her sleep was disturbed by strange dreams. In her dreams, she saw something beneath the tree. In her waking hours, she grew more and more curious. Her husband argued with her; he knew it was his job to protect the tree, no matter what, and he tried to persuade his wife to leave the tree alone. The woman would not listen, though, and finally, she decided to dig around the tree's roots. She uprooted the tree and found an enormous opening beneath it. She leaned over for a closer look. As she did so, her husband gave her a push!

The woman tumbled down and down. The wind whistled past her, and she could hear the sound of many waters.

The beneath world was covered with water at this time. Water beings

This mobile sculpture is in the Iroquois Indian Museum near Howe Caverns, New York. The waterfowl and turtle's back are seen as visitors descend a flight of stairs—reminding them of what Sky Woman would have seen in her fall from the Sky World.

lived there, and the waterfowl, floating on top of the vast ocean, looked up and saw the Sky Woman fall. They sped beneath her and snatched her in their beaks.

An enormous snapping turtle happened to be rising to the top of the water. Seeing how frail the woman was, the fowl asked the Great Turtle if he would bear the woman on his back. He agreed, and the animals gathered around the strange two-legged creature and talked kindly to her.

Sky Woman told them about the above world and everything up there. She described the earth and how she missed having ground underneath her feet. The water creatures had heard that soil lay underneath their water world. Determined to help the two-legged one, the various animals went to get mud from beneath the great waters. Each in turn, the creatures dove toward the bottom. None could dive deep enough. Finally, Little Toad dove for the bottom. When he surfaced, his mouth was full of mud.

The animals took this precious bit of soil and placed it on the back of the Great Turtle. The woman was elated. She began to dance in what today we call a counterclockwise direction, and the mud grew and spread over the turtle's back. As she danced and danced, the mud grew and grew until it became the land we now call North America. (That is why today the Haudenosaunee still dance in that same direction.) Sky Woman sprinkled dust into the air, and it turned into twinkling stars. Next, she created Sun and Moon.

The time came when Sky Woman was ready to give birth to her child—a daughter. Over time, the child grew into a beautiful woman. One night, as the daughter lay sleeping, the Spirit of the West Wind visited her. He lay two arrows on her chest—one sharp and one blunt. When she awoke, she

Key Words at a Glance

Haudenosaunee
Pronounced: "ho-deh-no-sho-nee"
"People of the Longhouse"
Importance: the six united Indian nations

Iroquois
Pronounced: "ear-uh-kwa"
"Snakes"
Importance: the Wyandotte name for the Six Nations, the name by which the Haudenosaunee are commonly known today.

The Three Sisters
corn, bean, and squash
Importance: the essential food plants that came from the Americas.

Iroquois today still feel a deep sense of connection to the earth and its plants and waters.

was pregnant. Her time came to deliver, and she gave birth to twins. The first birth was easy, and that twin was beautiful to look at. The second twin didn't come out the right way; he tore his mother's body, and she died as soon as he was born. This twin was ugly and grew to be evil.

Sky Woman grieved and buried her daughter. Her deceased daughter was known from then on as "Mother Earth." From the place she was buried grew three plants. They are called "the Three Sisters": corn, bean, and squash. When the white people came to the Great Turtle Land, the Indians shared these plants with them, and now the whole world feeds on these gifts from Mother Earth. From Mother Earth's heart grew another plant—tobacco. That is why the Haudenosaunee and other Native people send prayers from their heart to the Creator using tobacco. From her face grew strawberries, which the people who have passed on to the next life enjoy forever. Other plants grew from her face, and these have power to heal illnesses. Many lives have been spared by Mother Earth's bounty.

One of the twins was named Sapling. He became kind and gentle as he grew. The other was named Flint, and his heart became hard and cold like his name. When grown, the twins began to create things. The things Sapling created were good. He made the four-legged people, who provide humans with their skins and meat for food. He made freshwater lakes and streams, and fish that are delicious to eat. In short, he made all things that bring health and pleasure on the back of the Great Turtle.

Everything Flint did was just the opposite from Sapling's acts. What Sapling made good, Flint tried to **subvert**. He put bones in fish that were hard to pick out. He put thorns on the berry bushes. He covered the world with freezing cold and snow—but Sapling fixed that so the winter would have to give way to spring each year. Flint created horrific monsters—but Sapling drove them beneath the earth. Sometimes these monsters try to break out, but the Thunder beings strike at them from the clouds and turn them to stone.

Sapling could not allow his evil brother to continue ruining the created world, so the two brothers fought against one another. It was a terrible contest, but in the end Sapling prevailed over his twin. Flint was a supernatural being, though, so he could not pass into the next world. He was driven beneath the earth's surface, but he remained on Great Turtle.

Sapling is known as Sonkwaiatison, the Creator. As we give thanks to him, he will continue to replenish Mother Earth. We must be respectful and care for Mother Earth. These are precious truths, and they show the right ways to the Haudenosaunee today.

Stone tools are the most common objects that remain from the earliest people who lived in northeastern North America. Shown here are axe heads and celts (axes without grooves). These are shaped by knocking or "pecking" rocks. In the middle and lower right are scrapers for cleaning hides. In the middle of the bottom row is a stone drill point. Drilling with this could make wampum beads. On the bottom left are a Folsom point and a Clovis point. Spear points like these were used more than 10,000 years ago to hunt giant game like wooly mammoths or mastodons. The points in this picture were made by Mike Tarbell, using ancient methods.

Chapter 2

History: The Great Peace and Attempts to Break It

Soon after Europeans arrived on the eastern shores of this continent, they encountered five great, united Indian nations. The Haudenosaunee inspired many of the customs all Americans enjoy today.

Haudenosaunee traditions say their people used to live in the southwestern states. The Hopi, who live in modern-day Arizona, are still referred to by the Haudenosaunee as "our cousins." Long ago, the Iroquois's ancestors *migrated* eastward and eventually settled in what is today New York State.

The long-ago Iroquois chiefs ruled like *dictators*. Tribes fought over the best fields, and the soil was covered with blood. Around the year 1100, a woman and her young daughter fled from the violence. They lived far from people, so it came as a surprise when the daughter became pregnant; the sacred traditions say she had never been with a man. Her special child came to be known as "the Peacemaker." When he reached manhood, he told his mother and grandmother that the Creator had a special purpose for his life: he was to establish a Great Peace.

He began his work among the Seneca. They had a powerful woman leader named Jikonsahseh. He told her, "Because you are the first to accept the Law of Peace, it shall be the *clan* mothers who choose the chiefs."

A peaceful man named Aiionwatha (commonly called Hiawatha) lived among the Onondaga. When a powerful sorcerer named Tadodaho *instigated* a riot, Aiionwatha's seven daughters were killed. Overwhelmed by grief, Aiionwatha wandered alone. He came to a dry lake bed and picked up snail shells, which he beaded on a string.

Peacemaker came upon Aiionwatha, and he spoke *consolation* to the grief-stricken father. Peacemaker explained his words with the shell beads Aiionwatha had gathered. This began the practice of wampum beads, which are used to this day as a sacred *memory device*. The Peacemaker told Aiionwatha, "Now that your mind is cleared, we will establish The Great Peace."

The Mohawks, Oneidas, Cayugas, and Senecas agreed. The Onondaga, who were under the influence of Tadodaho, resisted. Aiionwatha and the Peacemaker went to Tadodaho, singing the song of peace. As they did so, the sorcerer's mind became good again. Recognizing the great influence Tadodaho held, the Peacemaker made him the central speaker for the Five Nations.

A great pine tree grew next to Onondaga Lake, and this was called the Great Tree of Peace. Beneath the tree, the chiefs of the new *confederacy* promised to uphold the Great Law of Peace for all time. Together, the Five Nations were thought of as a great Longhouse.

At the time when Europeans invaded North America, the Haudenosaunee were one of the strongest cultures north of Mexico. Corn was the most important part of their diet. They fished and hunted. Medicine men knew how to use more than a hundred natural medicines for healing. Their hearty lifestyle made the Haudenosaunee taller and healthier than many Europeans were at that time.

Social structure was centered in the longhouses. These were constructed around a wooden framework, covered with elm bark. A clan occupied each longhouse. Villages were built as planned communities, surrounded by walls of tree posts.

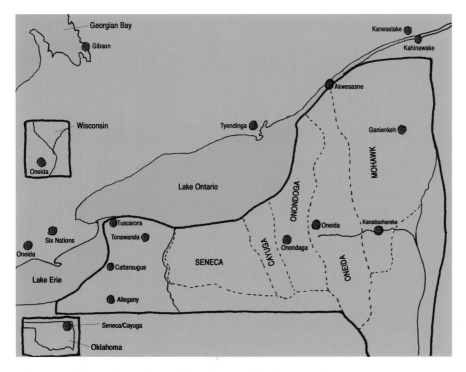

This map shows the traditional locations of the five Haudenosaunee nations. They were joined by the Tuscarora, forming Six Nations, in 1711. The Iroquois Confederacy was understood metaphorically as a longhouse, with the Mohawk guarding the Eastern Door and the Seneca the Western.

Altogether, the Five Nations controlled 24 million acres (9.7 million hectares) of land. Although European explorers referred to this as "wilderness," it was actually carefully managed. Forests were routinely burned with controlled fires to reduce underbrush. Trails and waterways were marked and cleared for travel.

Not all people wished to be part of the Great Peace, so the Five Nations waged war with other tribes. Haudenosaunee warriors wore elm bark armor, which repelled enemy arrows. They traveled swiftly in war canoes that held thirty or forty men. Their enemies feared them.

When Jacques Cartier and his crew arrived, starving and sick, the

Steel markers at the ancient village of Caughnawaga site show where wooden posts, around twelve feet high, were placed to form a double wall of protection around the village. When Europeans saw these fortified Haudenosaunee villages, they referred to them as "castles."

Mohawks welcomed these first Europeans to reach their lands and gave them food and medicine. In return, Cartier kidnapped some Mohawks and took them as slaves to Europe. Samuel de Champlain arrived in 1608 and attacked the Mohawks. In 1624, Dutch soldiers, allied with Mohican Indians, attacked the Mohawks. In response to these attacks, the Mohawks presented the Dutch government with a wampum (clamshell) belt, which portrayed two broad rivers flowing next to each other. This symbolized their desire for European and Haudenosaunee cultures to exist side by side, without conflict.

In the 1600s, French Catholic missionaries came to live among the Haudenosaunee. The People of the Longhouse welcomed them. Some Haudenosaunee were interested in the *economic* advantages that came from learning Christian ways; others were genuinely interested in the new faith. In 1676, a Mohawk girl named Kateri Tekakwitha was baptized. Kateri could not have imagined that hundreds of years later she would be revered as a saint.

In 1711, the Tuscarora Indians in North Carolina attacked the English and were defeated. The Tuscarora fled north, and in 1722, they were accepted as the Sixth Nation of the Haudenosaunee confederacy.

In the early 1700s, the Haudenosaunee established relationships with English settlers. They were interested in European ways, but they found their own traditions more useful and practical. Onondaga chief Canasetego explained in 1740:

> Several of our young people went to your colleges. When they came back to us, they were ignorant of every means of living in the woods, knew nothing of how to build shelter, take a deer or kill an enemy; were neither fit for hunters, warriors, or counselors—they were totally good for nothing.

The French and English fought each other between 1754 and 1763, and the Haudenosaunee allied with the French. After the French were defeated, the English government tried to settle with the Indians. The Royal Proclamation of 1763 promised a permanent "Indian Territory" west of the thirteen colonies. England guaranteed that settlers would not be

Burying the Hatchets

"A pine tree has been pulled up from the ground and into the hole beneath it we throw all weapons of war. Now strong currents of water shall carry them far away. We will now replace the pine tree sealing the burial of our weapons to establish the Great Law. Trouble between each other will now cease and the Haudenosaunee will keep the Great Law."

—the Peacemaker's Declaration establishing the Great Peace

allowed to move there. This new agreement did not sit well with the King's subjects in the American colonies. They wanted more land. Settlers kept moving into Haudenosaunee territory. Colonial desire to take over Indian lands was a major motivation for war against England—the Revolutionary War.

The Six Nations were about to be tested severely. They would be able to withstand the challenge they faced only if they stayed united. When the Peacemaker brought the Great Peace, he took five arrows and showed how difficult they were to break when gathered in a bundle. If they were divided, the Iroquois could be defeated.

As soon as the English colonies revolted, both sides ran to the Haudenosaunee seeking their help. Hanyery was an Oneida chief, whose father was a German colonist. Joseph Brant was a Mohawk warrior, whose sister was married to an English Indian agent. German settlers and English officials had been feuding a long time. Hanyery and the Oneida people he led allied with the American colonists, and Brant led the Mohawks to fight for England. At the battle of Oriskany, in 1777, the Great Peace was shattered. In the service of foreign nations, the Haudenosaunee fought against one another.

George Washington ordered General John Sullivan to take a large army up the Susquehanna River and *decimate* Indian villages along the way. The Mohawks gave President Washington a nickname: "Town Destroyer." On August 29, 1777, General Sullivan's army decisively defeated the Seneca at Newtown, New York. Following this campaign, the Continental Army distributed blankets to the defeated Indians, blankets that had been taken from victims of *smallpox*. This early example of germ warfare spread a dreadful disease to ensure that the Seneca would be further weakened.

The People of the Longhouse now faced a time of crisis. Settlers swarmed over their lands. European diseases decimated them. The Haudenosaunee desperately needed something to give them hope.

Handsome Lake was a Seneca who brought that hope to the Iroquois people. As a young man, he drank heavily. But in 1799, during an illness, he received a vision: the Creator had allowed the Haudenosaunee people to suffer because they had turned away from right living. Handsome Lake had other visions and received instructions on how to live right. His message became known as the Code of Handsome Lake, or Longhouse

Kateri Tekakwitha was baptized as a young woman in 1676. She has been beatified—recognized as especially holy—by the Catholic Church, and thousands of Catholics ask for her assistance in prayer. This shrine is at her childhood home of Caughnawaga.

Religion. These teachings encouraged great numbers of Haudenosaunee to keep traditional ways. His teachings are still very important for the Iroquois.

In the 1800s, women of the Six Nations played a vital role in women's rights everywhere. The first women's conference at Seneca Falls in 1848 reflected the inspiration of Seneca women. Two of the three founders of America's early *feminism* had spent time in Haudenosaunee society. In a time when American women were regarded as their husbands' legal property, the power of Haudenosaunee women was an eye-opener to many American women. In 1914, six years before women had the right to vote, a

The Iroquois Indian Museum was built in the shape of a longhouse. The longhouse is an important metaphor for the Haudenosaunee people, referring to their traditional housing, to the confederation, and to their governmental structure and spiritual beliefs.

This headdress, made in the 1930s, is traditional Haudenosaunee style. The arrangement of the eagle feather on top signifies which nation the wearer belongs to. One eagle feather on top shows the wearer is Seneca. Such headdresses are still worn for special ceremonies. Chiefs wear antlers in theirs.

magazine cartoon portrayed Indian women watching a parade for women's **suffrage**. A verse under the print read:

> We, the women of the Iroquois
> Own the Land, the Lodge, the Children
> Ours is the right to adoption, life or death;
> Ours is the right to raise up and depose chiefs;
> Ours is the right to *representation* in all councils;
> Ours is the right to make and *abrogate* treaties;
> Ours is the supervision over *domestic* and foreign policies;
> Ours is the *trusteeship* of tribal property;
> Our lives are valued as high as man's.

61 - 73 FOX CREEK POINTS

If you walk through farm fields next to rivers in upstate New York, you can find chert projectile points like these, lying in the dirt. They remind us that this land was inhabited for thousands of years before Europeans came. Some of these may be older than the time when the Five Nations arrived in the state. Always make sure you have the owner's permission before you hunt for artifacts! Write down where you find any artifacts, as such information may help archaeologists understand the story of ancient life in your part of the country.

The ancient Mohawk village site of Caughnawaga near Fonda, New York, is the largest Haudenosaunee archaeological site to be excavated. If you look from front to back of the markers you can get a sense of how large this village was. Catholics revere the ancient village of Caughnawaga as the childhood home of Kateri Tekakwitha. There is another Mohawk village with this name today near Montreal, Quebec.

American women who enjoy equal rights with men today can thank their Haudenosaunee sisters.

The People of the Longhouse continued to fight for their rights as the twentieth century began. Deskaheh, a Cayuga chief in Canada, was an important leader of the struggle. When the Canadian government began taking away tribal rights in 1921, he traveled to England to plead his case on behalf of the Six Nations. He was unsuccessful, but the Six Nations became known internationally.

This painting by Bert Smith is dedicated to the Skywalkers—Iroquois men who worked on the high steel, building much of New York City.

These stone arrowheads were made by Mike Tarbell. The antler billet (hammer) is used to strike flakes off quartz or chert stones to make the points. The traditional bow is a fine tool for hunting—powerful, accurate, and silent. Though bullets were much more damaging, Native people continued to use the bow for a long time alongside guns. Europeans hired Indians to hunt for them since Native people were highly skilled at stalking.

In the 1930s, during the **Great Depression**, Haudenosaunee people had few jobs. When the Canadian government began building bridges, they discovered the men of the Six Nations were willing to undertake this dangerous work; what's more, they excelled at it and their fame spread across the border to America. Mohawk steelworkers became legendary for their work in New York City, where they were referred to as "skywalkers." Many Iroquois helped build the World Trade Center. After the tragic attack on September 11, 2001, Iroquois workers rushed to help.

In both World Wars, as well as the conflicts in Korea and Vietnam, the Six Nations fought bravely. Both in Canada and the United States, a higher percentage of Indians volunteered for service than any other ethnic group. Some modern-day Mohawk warriors had their military haircuts shaved in the style of their ancestors.

The 1960s and 1970s brought a new sense of pride in Indian communities throughout America. Ray Fadden, a prominent Iroquois, reminded the Haudenosaunee how much they had contributed to the world. Tom Porter led efforts to revitalize the Mohawk language. Chief Jake Swamp and others became involved in the American Indian Movement.

In the 1990s, the Haudenosaunee experienced a series of contests with outside governments. The Senecas burned tires, shutting down a major interstate freeway, when the New York government insisted on taxing reservation sales. There was also friction within the Nations themselves. Akwasasne, which borders the United States and Canada, saw conflicts between Iroquois *traditionalists* and business interests. Illegal smuggling of cigarettes, alcohol, as well as the transportation of illegal aliens from

The flag of the Haudenosaunee Confederacy, the original "united nations," is taken from the image of the Hiawatha (Aiionwatha) Wampum Belt. It portrays the council fires of the five original tribes, joined together in unity with the Great Tree of Peace at Onondaga in the middle.

Canada to the United States through the reservation added to the tension. Onondaga and Oneida Nations also experienced confrontations between rival factions.

The greatest dreams are hardest to achieve. The Six Nations have not always been able to live out the Great Peace. Nonetheless, they have had considerable influence on world history. We North Americans who enjoy freedom, equality, and peace today owe much to the example of the original United Nations—the Haudenosaunee.

This stained glass window is in the Shako:wi Oneida Cultural Center. The Great White Pine Tree of Peace is in the center. It is surrounded by the wolf, turtle, and bear—the three clans of the Oneida. The eagle in the tree watches for threats to the six nations. In his talons he holds a wampum belt with six purple squares representing the nations of the Haudenosaunee confederacy.

Chapter 3

Current Government

In social studies class you have probably learned how representatives are elected from each community to represent citizens. You may see reports on the news about how the United Nations is working for world peace. What you may not know is that the Haudenosaunee began many of the political freedoms you enjoy today.

When the founding fathers of the United States met to write a *constitution* in 1787, a number of them were familiar with the Haudenosaunee system of government. In 1754, Benjamin Franklin sat in council with the chiefs of the Six Nations and carefully wrote down what he learned about their way of government. Just before the Constitutional Convention, Franklin and others were working to create the shape of an Iroquois-style government for the new nation. The Iroquois system was a model for America's national government.

Brian Patterson is a modern-day council member of the Oneida Nation. He explains that the Oneida have nine chiefs, or *hoyane*. These nine represent the Oneidas at the Grand Council of the Six Nations. The Oneida also have three appointed members of the Tribal Council. The clan mothers

Brian Patterson is a council member of the Oneida Nation.

select both the chiefs and the councilmen. Brian says, "The clan mothers are the heart and soul of our nation, the true leaders of our people."

Brian is a tall, pleasant man in his thirties. Like many Indians today, he sports a long ponytail. Brian never thought he'd want to be in politics, so he never sought his council position—which is probably why he was chosen. The clan mothers choose people who are humble and not self-seeking.

On Mondays, Brian meets with the council in an *executive* session. On Tuesdays, meetings are held in the council house; these meetings are open to anyone who wants to come. Tribal members sit with their clans. Anyone can raise an issue. The clan mothers sit with the councilmen and chiefs and discuss issues with them. The clan mothers don't vote, but they hold power to remove the councilmen if they feel they are being irresponsible— so the men think about what they say in meetings! Ordinarily, the chiefs and councilmen serve for life.

Brian says the most fulfilling part of being a councilman is making sure

Oneida Nation Council members stand together with Indian ironworkers who are working on the expansion of Turning Stone Casino in Verona, New York.

Funds from tribal business ventures have enabled the Oneida Nation to provide many services for members.

Chief Material

When the clan mothers consider who should serve as "Hoyaneh," or clan chief, they look for these qualities:

    pleasant personality
    honesty
    no criminal record
    wisdom
    knowledge of traditional laws
    knowledge of traditional spiritual
        ways
    faithfulness to his family
    ability to uphold the Great Law of
        Peace
    ability to represent others fairly
    kindness
    ability to take criticism

the Oneida culture is not lost for future generations. He has been privileged to help with **repatriation**. For instance, a woman called and said she had wampum belts that had been in her family for years. She used to "play Indian" with them as a child. She wondered if the tribe would like to have them. One of the elders, a Cayuga chief who has since died, came to "read" the wampum belt. On one belt were nine squares, representing nine council fires. This gave the modern tribe an important message from the past. As Brian says, the Peacemaker's message was very **inclusive** and additional nations joined the confederacy in the past. As cultural objects are returned to the Haudenosaunee, the modern Iroquois Nation is enriched.

Brian Patterson's councilman role is a modern addition to the organization of the Six Nations. The chiefs, representing each clan, are a tradition dating back to 1142 when the Great Peace was established. Each nation (or tribe) is divided into clans. Each clan selects a chief, or hoyaneh. These are called "Caretakers of the Peace." The clan mothers meet and decide whom they will put forward as chief. The people of the clan then meet and either approve or reject their choice. There is no "head chief" in the Nation, and the tribal council of chiefs operates by consensus rather than majority vote. This ancient method of decision making is becoming popular in the business world today.

At regular intervals, the chiefs of the Six Nations meet together in the Grand Council at Onondaga, the capital of the Confederacy. The large log building in which they meet is referred to as the Longhouse. There are fifty chiefs when all are gathered, representing all the clans of all the nations. The clan chiefs thus serve like congressmen or representatives in the U.S. Congress. The chiefs resolve disputes and plan for the welfare of all the people. When they meet in Grand Council, the chiefs divide into sections: Elder Brothers and Younger Brothers, similar to the U.S. government's two-house legislature. In the U.S. government, executive power is vested

Terms at a Glance

Hoyane—chiefs who represent their clan. (*Hoyaneh* is the singular form of the word.)

The Grand Council—the gathering of all chiefs from all Six Nations of the Haudenosaunee.

Carson Waterman made this painting of clan mothers, the powerful women who nominate chiefs and weigh what is said in council. The clan mothers in the picture are each holding one of the "Three Sisters"—corn, beans, and squash.

The Onondaga Longhouse is the heart of the Haudenosaunee Confederacy, where the Grand Council meets.

in the president. In the Iroquois Grand Council, the chiefs choose one of themselves to be the "Onondaga." The Onondaga has the final say as to whether a matter has been confirmed or denied.

This system is the world's oldest continuing representative democracy. It has faced more than a few challenges in the modern world. The original form of government is still in place at some Iroquois villages. At others, such as Oneida, there are both traditional chiefs and additional council

Really Thick Skin

According to Iroquois tradition, leaders must have skin "seven layers thick." In other words, they must have great ability to receive criticism and not be angered.

members. In other villages, the clans still exist, but chiefs lack actual political power.

It is sometimes difficult to balance traditional governments and modern economic demands. In the mid-1980s, the Wolf Clan mothers selected Ray Halbritter, a Harvard-educated Oneida businessman, as chief representing the clan. In 1993, Chief Halbritter negotiated the opening of Turning Stone Casino, a highly successful economic move for the tribe. Income from the casino pays for many of the community improvements appreciated by the Oneida today. However, many traditional Iroquois oppose gambling. They do not believe their people should profit from a casino. Today the federal government of the United States recognizes Ray Halbritter as Oneida chief—but the Grand Council does not.

Modern realities present other challenges for the Peacemaker's vision of the Great Peace. And yet the Peacemaker's ideas have endured for nine hundred years. They influenced the birth of modern democracy in America and consequently throughout the world. No other government can make such a boast.

Mike Tarbell, educator at the Iroquois Indian Museum, enjoys sharing his Mohawk culture with guests.

Chapter 4

Today's Spiritual Beliefs

Mike Tarbell grew up influenced by both **Western** and Iroquois ways. His father urged him to do well in school and go to college. His mother was steeped in traditional ways, and her mother was a *medicine woman*. As a child, Mike spent a great deal of time learning about the sacred teachings and natural medicines from her.

After graduation, Mike "worked the high steel" for a time, building bridges and buildings, then enlisted in the military, where he did two tours in Vietnam. On his second tour, he was sent to work with the people of a Vietnamese mountain tribe. They slept in longhouses and enjoyed a quiet fire at night while listening to the calls of wild creatures in the forest. Mike felt right at home.

While his time with the mountain people enabled him to feel connected with himself, he also had horrific experiences in Vietnam. Returning home, he struggled with *post-traumatic stress disorder*. He took courses in college and went through various programs to help him, but the most important healing came through the ways of his people.

For centuries, the Mohawk have practiced a cleansing ceremony for warriors returning to the longhouse after battle. After Mike's return from Vietnam, a group of friends and relatives called his father and told him to bring Mike to an event where Tom Porter was speaking. The whole family went. Mike was led to a chair in the middle of the group. He sat down, and a blanket was placed on him. When he realized what was happening, he asked, "Can my dad sit with me here?" His dad had been a paratrooper in World War II, and Mike knew his father also still suffered from his war memories. So father and son received the healing ceremony together.

This was the beginning of Mike's healing. Later, he began to work as an educator at the Iroquois Indian Museum near Howe's Caverns in New York State. When Mike first walked into the museum longhouse, an old man saw him coming through the door and said, "You've been running in the woods." This expression meant that Mike had been feeling lost. "It's time to come home," the old man continued. The old man's insight encouraged Mike to continue his healing through the traditions of his people. He went to a clan mother he knew and she gave him some medicine to drink. He had a dream with powerful spiritual importance. This happened several times.

Today, Mike is a confident and appealing speaker as he shares about Haudenosaunee ways with visitors at the museum. He has met many other Vietnam veterans in his job, and he has been glad to encourage them to find peace in their lives. Mike knows he has also benefited from the education his father encouraged, but he finds wholeness following the ancestral beliefs of his Mohawk people.

For a long time, many non-Indians studied Native beliefs in order to *suppress* Indian practices, or to try and show the superiority of Western ideas. As a result, many Indians are reluctant to share details about their spiritual practices, knowing sacred teachings can be easily misunderstood or abused.

Thanksgiving is at the heart of Longhouse spirituality. Many members of the Six Nations begin each day by reciting "Words That Come Before All Else." This thanksgiving helps to keep a "good mind"—an attitude of gratitude and peace.

Longhouse spirituality involves a continual cycle of thanksgiving. Elaborate ceremonies remind the people of their role as caretakers of Mother Earth. Ceremonies take place within the Longhouse, and "Faithkeepers"

Prayer Honoring Kateri Tekakwitha

Lord God, You called the virgin Blessed Kateri Tekakwitha to shine among the American Indian people as an example of innocence of life. Through her intercession, may all peoples of every tribe, tongue, and nation, having been gathered into Your Church, proclaim Your greatness in one song of praise. We ask this through our Lord Jesus Christ, Your Son, who lives and reigns with You and the Holy Spirit, one God, forever and ever. Amen.

From the Catholic prayer for services honoring Kateri Tekakwitha.

The Roman Catholic Church honors Kateri Tekakwitha as the patroness of ecology and the environment.

within each clan guard the traditions. The sacred festivals of thanksgiving are:

Midwinter Thanksgiving
Maple Thanksgiving
Thunder Thanksgiving
Seed Thanksgiving
Strawberry Thanksgiving
Corn Planting Thanksgiving
Corn Hoeing Thanksgiving
Little Festival of Green Corn
Great Festival of Ripe Corn
Complete Thanksgiving for the Harvest

The Seneca prophet Handsome Lake revived the strength of the Six Nations. His grave is on the Onondaga Nation, just south of Syracuse, New York.

The annual schedule of Haudenosaunee thanksgiving festivals includes celebrations of planting, hoeing, and harvesting corn.

In chapter two, we discussed Handsome Lake, who revived the strength of the Six Nations in the early 1800s. His spiritual teachings are still followed by the majority of people in the Six Nations. The Code of Handsome Lake begins by warning against three practices—drunkenness, sorcery, and abortion. Next come many practical instructions regarding healthy marriages and families. If couples are always fighting bitterly, for example, and they do not have children, Handsome Lake believed they would be better living apart. If they have children, he taught that they must learn to get along better. Food must be shared with guests, whether one is prepared for them or not. Children are not to be punished by spanking; a really bad child is splashed with cold water. Parents must not favor one child over another. Handsome Lake also gave teachings about many everyday relationships. "Everyone has been given a gift of one sort or another by the

Jonathan Maracle and his Broken Walls Ministry express Christian beliefs using Native North American musical styles.

Creator," he said, "and they should be respectful of these things and respect other people as well." Pets are to be treated kindly as well.

Handsome Lake gave many prophecies also. He predicted "a form of transportation that will not be pulled by a horse or pushed by anything. Many people will enjoy this form of transportation, and many will die from it." He predicted changes in the world's climate and ecological damage. Many of his predictions have come true.

Traditional medicine societies are still important for the Haudenosaunee today. In 1995, the Grand Council of the Six Nations issued this statement:

> Within the Haudenosaunee there are various medicine societies that have the sacred duty to maintain the use and strength of special medicines, both for individual and community welfare. A medicine society is comprised of Haudenosaunee who have partaken of the medicine and are thereby bound to the protection and perpetuation of the special medicines. Such medicines are essential to the spiritual and emotional well-being of the Haudenosaunee communities.
>
> Among these medicine societies are those that utilize the wooden masks and corn husk masks, which represent the shared power of the original medicine beings. All the masks have power and an intended purpose that is solely for the members of the respective medicine societies. Interference with the sacred duties of the societies and/or their masks is a violation of the freedom of the Haudenosaunee and does great harm to the welfare of the Haudenosaunee communities.
>
> The mask is sacred and is only to be used for its intended purpose. Masks should not be made unless they are to be used by members of the medicine society, according to established tradition.

Not all Haudenosaunee people follow Longhouse Religion; there are also many Christians in the Six Nations. Jonathan Maracle, for example, grew up in Akwesasne Mohawk Territory, and his father, Andrew Maracle Sr., was a Christian who translated church music from English to the Mohawk language. As a child, Jonathan often heard his father singing these songs. Jonathan later moved to Ontario and started a band. When his music became popular, Jonathan decided to move to California. On the West Coast, his band played onstage with Peter Frampton, Dokken, and other well-known musical groups. At a very low time in his life, Jonathan experienced "a personal relationship with God."

"The Words Before All Else"
The Great Prayer of Thanksgiving

Variations of this prayer all follow the same outline. The version below has been paraphrased from a Mohawk version.

We bring our minds together as we give greetings and thanks to each other.

We thank Mother Earth, for she gives us all that we need for life.

We give thanks to all the waters of the world for quenching our thirst and giving us life.

We thank all the fish who purify the water and give themselves to us as food.

We thank all the wild plants who feed all life on the earth.

With one mind, we turn to honor and thank all the food plants we harvest from the garden. Since the beginning of time, they have enabled the people to survive.

We thank the medicine plants who are always waiting and ready to heal us.

We thank all the animals who have so many things to teach us.

With one mind, we greet and thank the trees who provide shelter, food, and many useful things.

We thank all the birds who remind us to enjoy and appreciate life.

We are thankful to the four winds. They come bringing us messages and giving us strength.

We thank the Thunder Beings who keep the evil monsters in their places beneath the earth.

We thank our eldest brother, the Sun. He is the source of all the fires of life.

We thank our oldest grandmother, the Moon, who lights the nighttime sky. She is the leader of women all over the world.

We give thanks to the stars who guide us at night.

We gather our minds to greet and thank the teachers who remind us of the way we were instructed to live as people.

Now we turn our thoughts to the Creator, or Great Spirit, and send greetings and thanks for all the gifts of creation and for all the love that is around us.

We now end our words. If something was forgotten, we leave it to each individual to give thanks in his or her own way.

Kay Olan enjoys a walk to the pond at Kanatsiohareke, in New York's Mohawk Valley. For Kay and many other Iroquois, nature inspires a sense of thanksgiving.

"In my world nothing ever really dies," says Mike Tarbell. "We don't have a word for death and dying. There are no good-byes. We will meet again, whether in this realm or in the land of strawberries, which is our heaven. John Lennon had it right when he wrote 'Strawberry Fields Forever.'" This mosaic-style acrylic painting by Marnie Tarbell is titled Strawberries.

According to the Broken Walls Ministries Web site:

Jonathan had heard Christian music from around the world and in most cases the message of the gospel had been conformed to the musical style of the country from which it came. After having lived on Native territories all of his life and never having heard Christ in **indigenous** Native music (in fact always thinking of them as opposites) there was quite a wall to be broken in Jonathan's own life to even consider mixing the two. In 1995 he was asked to sing the Mohawk Chant on the 1995 *March for Jesus* album. Shortly after, he was inspired to create music which would break down barriers: barriers between English, French, and Indian people, and barriers between different Christian church groups. He and his family dance, play the flute, and sing songs in English and Mohawk. Jonathan calls his group "Broken Walls Ministries." They have performed all over the world.

The Mohawks may also soon be the only North American Indian nation to claim their own Catholic saint. The Catholic Church honors Kateri Tekakwitha as the patroness of ecology and the environment. The daughter of a Mohawk chief, she was born in upstate New York in 1656. When she was four years old, smallpox attacked her village, taking the lives of her parents and leaving Tekakwitha permanently scarred. When Kateri was eighteen a French Catholic missionary came to her village, and she was baptized that Easter. Her family wanted her to marry, but she wanted to be totally committed to Christ, so she left her home and traveled to Canada where there was a village of Christian Indians. She died from an illness when she was only twenty-four. Her last words were "Jesus, I love you." Two priests who were with her when she died claimed her badly scarred face immediately became smooth. She was *beatified* in 1980 by Pope John Paul II. Catholic Indians all over America seek her help in prayer.

As you can see from this chapter, modern Iroquois worship in a variety of ways. Some are Catholic, others are Protestants, and many live by Longhouse beliefs. Whatever form it takes, spiritual life is very important to the Haudenosaunee today.

This life-size clay sculpture by Tammy Tarbell-Boehning (Mike Tarbell's sister) is titled Iroquois Woman. *Western women today are just beginning to enjoy the equalities long held by their sisters in the Six Nations.*

Chapter 5

Social Structures Today

In Doug George-Kanentiio's book *Iroquois Culture and Commentary*, he tells a moving story titled "My Heroine, My Grandmother."

Her name was Josephine—Wari:so:se in the language of her own people. She lived on the reservation at Akwesasne, which straddles the border between Ontario and New York State, but times were hard, and her husband Jacob George often had to work outside the reservation in both New York and Ontario. They had nine children, who were a constant challenge to feed in the years before unemployment insurance, Welfare payments, or reservation distribution of casino moneys. In Josephine's day, people had to provide for themselves, so she did whatever she could: scaled fish, smoked meat, and spent hours by gas lamplight sewing clothes for the children.

George-Kanentiio writes that "in October of 1951 Wari:so:se passed into the spirit world in a way that caused great sorrow to her family but was marked with dignity, self-sacrifice, and honor." While she was visiting her daughter in Syracuse to help care for a newborn granddaughter, a fire broke out in the apartment building. Wari:so:se was told to leave, but she refused to leave the apartment without the baby. She reached the child but was cut off from escape by smoke and flame. Wari:so:se called from the window until people were in place, and then she carefully dropped her granddaughter safely into waiting arms below. Wari:so:se followed, but she died in the fall. Doug George-Kanentiio concludes, "Through her the present generation lives on. There is more than a little of Wari:so:se in our hearts and minds today."

The people of the Six Nations give special honor to elders and clan mothers. Women play important roles in their culture.

Although blatant *sexism* is less common than it used to be, many men in North American society are still uncomfortable giving women the credit they deserve. For example, they may resent working for a female boss. If a boy is close to his mother, paying attention to her guidance, he is sometimes teased for being a "mama's boy."

None of these are problems in Haudenosaunee culture. For healing and wisdom, men seek out clan mothers and medicine women. The clan mothers sit and weigh the decisions of male council members. Mothers, aunts,

---

Also Respect Your Nonhuman Family Members

"The creator told them, All the living creatures are your relations, and they all have instructions as to how they must live in this world. The natural life will always be ready to assist the living beings, if they live in harmony with one another. The humans must always look after their relations of the natural world."

From *Traditional Teachings*, by the North American Indian Traveling College.

Travis Cook, director of recreation for the Oneida Nation, coaches youth at a lacrosse clinic.

and grandmothers are highly esteemed by men of all ages. They are **revered** as givers and nurturers of life, even as Mother Earth maintains all of life.

The mother determines family relationships. As long as a mother is a member of a tribal nation, her children share tribal membership. If the mother is not a tribal member, even if the father is, the children will not be considered to be members of the tribe.

By the same token, children are honored in Iroquois society, as they represent the future of the Nations. Entire families—grandparents, aunts, and uncles—are involved in raising a child. The Iroquois believe that everyone is born with a particular gift, so adults watch toddlers carefully to see if they are mechanically skilled, musically talented, or show some

This painting by Carson Waterman portrays a mother of the Heron Clan.

other talent or skill. Parents must be careful to steer their children in the direction the Creator intended specifically for each one. If a family follows the Longhouse spiritual beliefs, the children will be given names in their native language. Christian families do not usually do this.

Clans are very important to the Six Nations, since family, political, social, and religious aspects of life are all related to clan. Because members of a clan are related, they cannot marry a member of the same clan. The number and names of clans vary between the Six Nations. Clans found among the Senecas are: Bear, Deer, Turtle, Snipe, Heron, Beaver, Wolf, and Hawk.

Originally the Six Nations were neatly arranged side by side across the state of New York, but now they are spread out more unevenly, from Canada to Oklahoma. What follows is a rough summary of where the Iroquois live today, and how many live where.

The Seneca, or *Onondowahgah* live on these reservations:

- Allegany Reservation is in Cattaraugus County, New York. It has 20,000 acres (about 8,000 hectares). The entire town of Salamanca is located within tribal borders, and non-Indian home owners and businesses lease the land on which they reside. More than a thousand Seneca live on the Allegany reservation.
- Cattaraugus Reservation, not far from the Allegany Reservation, has 21,000 acres (about 8,500 hectares) and a population of more than two thousand.
- Oil Springs Reservation near Cuba, New York, was created to protect a sacred mineral spring. It is only a single square mile (2.89 square kilometers), with no permanent residents.
- Tonawanda Reservation in Erie County, New York, consists of 7,550 acres (about 3,000 hectares), but only a quarter of that is tribally owned. Tribal population is 453.
- Six Nations Reservation in Ontario, Canada, boasts a population of 9,500.
- The Seneca-Cayuga Reservation is located in Ottawa County, Oklahoma. It has approximately eight hundred members.

The Cayuga or *Guyohkohnyoh* have no reservations. They were recently paid what they regard as a ridiculously small sum for the value of what used to be their land. They live with the Seneca and Onondaga on their

Kellie Confer (Turtle Clan) is a teacher assistant at the Oneida Nation's Early Learning Center. She is playing with Elijah Bandera (Turtle Clan) and Aliyah Frederick (Turtle Clan). Children are honored in Haudenosaunee society as they represent the future of the Nations.

reservations. They have kept their clans, clan mothers, chiefs, and place at the Great Assembly.

The Onondaga or *Onundagaono* have these reservations:

- The Onondaga Reservation is just south of Syracuse, New York. It contains 7,300 acres (about 3,000 hectares), all tribally owned. There are 1,600 tribal members.
- Six Nations Reservation contains three thousand Onondaga.

Next, the Oneida or *Onayotekaono* have the following reservations:

- The Oneida Reservation is located in Brown and Outagamie Counties, Wisconsin. It contains 2,500 acres (about 1,000 hectares), but non-Indians have purchased most of the land. There are 2,500 Oneida residents living on the Oneida Reservation.
- The New York Oneida community owns 32 acres (13 hectares) in Madison County, near the city of Oneida. It is not a reservation, but

the land is tribally owned. There are only thirty-seven residents, but seven hundred live in nearby communities.

- Some Oneida live on the Onondaga Reservation.

The Mohawk or *Kanienka:haka* live in these areas:

- Kahnawake/Caughnawaga and Doncaster Reserves are in Canada. Kahnawake means "At the Rapids," referring to the Lachine Rapids near Montreal, Quebec. The reserves contain about 12,000 and 20,000 acres (about 5,000 and 8,000 hectares) of land. The population is approximately eight thousand.
- Oka/Kanesatake/Lake of Two Mountains in Quebec, Canada, is roughly 39 square miles (111 square kilometers) in size. It is mostly populated by Algonquin Indians, but 1,800 Mohawks also live there.
- Gibson Reserve, Ontario, Canada, is home to eight hundred Mohawks.
- St. Regis Reservation/Akwesasne Reserve straddles Franklin County, New York, and Ontario, Canada. Akwesasne means "The Land Where the Partridge Drums." It contains 14,600 acres (about 5,900 hectares). Around 1,900 Mohawks live on the reserve.
- Many Mohawks also live on Six Nations/Grand River Reservation in Ontario, Canada.
- Tyendinega Reserve, also called Deseronto, is in Ontario, Canada. Around three thousand Mohawks live there.
- Ganienkeh Reservation in Altoona, New York, is home to three hundred Mohawks.
- Brooklyn, New York (in New York City), is home to many Mohawks.
- Kanatsiohareke is a small Mohawk community in New York's Mohawk Valley. The residents are committed to living by traditional values in their ancestral homeland.

The Six Nations have worked hard to improve their economic situation. They have invested in business opportunities, and they are better off financially than some other Indian groups.

Many Iroquois live in frame houses. Some live in double-wide manufac-

A tribally owned service station at the Seneca Nation in Salamanca, New York.

tured homes, and some live in trailer homes. A few old log cabins can still be seen on the reservations, with tin roofs added.

Families often keep gardens to grow vegetables or herbs, and a few own farms. Yards are frequently left in their natural state, rather than mowed and trimmed.

Most reservations have many small businesses such as hardware stores, auto shops, and beauty shops. Smoke shops and gas stations are common, since tribal sales are not required to pay state sales taxes. Cigarette shops on tribal lands do a brisk business selling on the Internet. Some rural reservations have lumber and construction businesses. Turning Stone Casino, owned by the Oneidas, is one of the largest businesses in New York State. The Senecas are also currently building a casino just off Interstate 86.

Every Iroquois reservation has a Catholic church, and each community also has a ceremonial longhouse for council and spiritual meetings. Many reservations also have Protestant churches.

The Six Nations people operate numerous museums and cultural centers. The Shako:wi Cultural Center, in Verona, New York, displays *artifacts*

Turning Stone Casino and related businesses have enabled the Oneida to return their share of federal Indian money to the government.

and artwork of the Oneida. The Seneca National Museum has a large collection of historical items, and the Iroquois Indian Museum in Howe Caverns, New York, has the largest collection of modern Iroquois art. Kanatsiohareke, in Fonda, New York, runs a gift shop with traditional and modern Indian art as well as a great many books and tapes on Mohawk ways.

Visiting these places is a good way to learn about Haudenosaunee culture. Take the most advantage of your visit and talk with hosts and interpreters. Meeting people and sharing your lives is one of the best ways to learn.

Warrior's Dream *is a limestone carving by Tom Huff, a Seneca-Cayuga of the Deer* Clan.

Chapter 6

Contemporary Arts

The Haudenosaunee have always been great storytellers. Most of their traditional ways have been handed down from person to person, from mouth to ear. According to the ancient proverb, however, a picture is worth a thousand words, so it should not be surprising that the People of the Longhouse have also produced outstanding artists.

You have to look at a piece of art and think about it before it starts talking to you. For instance, Birdy Burdeck has in her office in the Shako:wi Cultural Center a picture she painted of a woman. At first you might just think it's a nice picture of an Indian woman. Then you learn more about it. This picture represents Birdy, her mother, and her grandmother and reflects the important role of elders in teaching the upcoming generations. The lips are her grandmother's because her grandmother always had wise things to say. The woman's nose and facial shape are those of Birdy's mother. This symbolizes the Oneida's system of family belonging, which is passed through the mother. The woman in the picture is holding a **smudge pot** and burning **white sage.** This means that prayer is going upward to the Creator. She is standing on Mother Earth, indicating her connection to the world of nature.

This painting by Birdy Burdeck portrays herself, her mother, and her grandmother, all in one image.

When you look carefully at the picture, you realize Birdy has communicated the most important elements of Haudenosaunee social structure and spiritual belief, along with the story of three generations in her own family. Yes, a picture is worth a thousand words.

Birdy got started as an artist when she was very young. Her mother gave her plaster-of-paris molds and some paint, and then directed her to paint the ceramics. While Birdy worked, she doodled on the paper that protected the table, and she discovered she enjoyed drawing more than painting the molds. Today, she never sketches before painting—she just starts painting with oils.

In long-ago times, the Six Nations used painting to decorate objects and record war exploits or clan affiliation. Easel painting did not begin until 1821. The earliest known Iroquois easel painter is Dennis Cusick, but by the early 1900s, there were a few other Iroquois painters as well.

Jesse Cornplanter is probably the most famous. Beginning in 1901, Cornplanter made sketches for Arthur Parker, the Seneca director of the Rochester Museum. While he was still in his early teens, Cornplanter was already a fine artist. His paintings are still important because they depict ordinary Iroquois life in his own day.

Ernest Smith of Tonawanda is perhaps the best-known contemporary painter from the Six Nations. He painted hundreds of pictures, and his art became popular before his death in 1975.

Painting as an art form has continued to flourish among the Haudenosaunee.

Wampum belts are art that has been telling stories for generations. Mike Tarbell, the educator at the Iroquois Indian Museum near Howe Caverns in New York State, calls wampum "bookmarks" in the Iroquois' oral tradition.

The flag of the Six Nations, for example, is a design taken from the famous Hiawatha Belt made from wampum. In the center of the belt is the Great Tree of Peace, representing both the Grand Council, which meets at

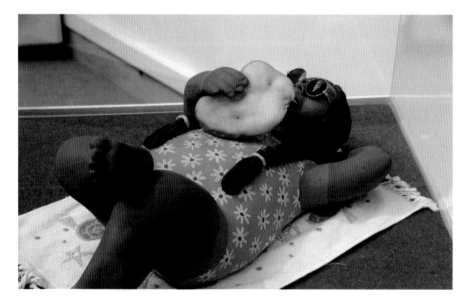

Freeda the Frybread Lady *is a humorous sculpture by Tammy Tarbell-Boehning. Her work can be seen in art shows and museums around the country.*

Onondaga, and the historical beginning of the Great Peace. Surrounding the tree are the lodge fires of the other nations, all connected together with a line showing their unity. The whole story of the Six Nations is tied together in that belt.

Julius Cook, of the Akwesasne Reservation, was a well-known silversmith. He also had the distinction of being the first Mohawk wampum belt maker in two hundred years. In 1998, Cook wove a replica of the famous Wolf Belt. He made it out of real quahog shell beads, the same type of shell used for wampum beads in the ancient past. Making the beads is a difficult, intricate task, a true labor of love. By doing so, Cook reestablished an art form that has been an essential part of Haudenosaunee identity for many generations. In Darren Bonaparte's article on Cook, written shortly after the artist's death, Bonaparte wrote:

> A person usually grows up to embody the meaning of their Mohawk name. Julius Cook's name was Sakaronhiokeweh, which means, "He Wipes the Sky." In my mind, Sakaronhiokeweh took the things the Creator perfected and somehow improved on them. This is the essence of what it means to be an artist or a craftsman, to take the things of nature and make them your own, to add your own "polish."

While wampum was used for recording sacred history, the Iroquois used tiny beads from European traders to ornament their clothing and bags. They developed a style of flower patterns, usually white beads on top of bright cloth backgrounds. The beads stand out from the material, giving a three-dimensional aspect to the art.

The word "wampum" is from the Narragansett word for "white shell beads." Indian people began making shell beads five thousand years ago. Wampum beads are made in two colors: white beads from the whelk shell and purple-black beads from the growth rings of the quahog clamshell. Wampum belts consist of rows of beads woven together. Belts were made on a simple loom.

European traders and politicians often used beads and trinkets to barter for Indian goods. Metal coins were scarce in New England, so wampum was used as currency. The use of wampum instead of money continued in the colonies until the American Revolution.

Carson Waterman's artwork is full of native symbols and images.

Samuel Thomas is an outstanding Iroquois beadwork artist. His Indian name is Kahdohdonh, which means "standing forest." He is Cayuga, of the Wolf Clan. He is especially noted for three-dimensional doves made from white beads on red cloth backgrounds. His beaded art is very intricate— each dove takes hundreds of tiny, individually threaded beads.

Another popular medium for Haudenosaunee artists is stone. For thousands of years, they have formed stone into useful yet artistic objects such as pendants and pipe bowls. In 1969, a Tuscarora artist named Duffy Wilson began carving in soapstone and met with great success. Many other Iroquois began to carve soapstone. The result was a remarkable new Iroquois art form.

Most carvers are men. Their works portray religious symbols, clan animals, or figures from ancient legends. Typical subjects are False Faces,

Tadodaho with snakes in his hair, the Tree of Peace, the Guardian Eagle, and other animals or people. Stone carvers feel very strongly about their work. They believe they are working in union with the stone itself. The resulting art communicates deep spiritual feelings.

Tom Huff is one of the best-known Iroquois soapstone sculptors. He works in a variety of styles, from traditional to contemporary. His art comments on the effects of American culture on Native Americans today. Tom believes stone is alive and has a spirit. He may spend weeks looking at a chunk of soapstone before determining what it will reveal.

Basketry is another traditional art form still practiced today. Basket making dates back centuries in Mohawk culture. Originally, baskets were used for everything from corn washing to berry picking. Beautiful "fancy" baskets were also made.

By the 1980s, the tradition of basket making was declining. The tradition was no longer being passed from generation to generation, and only a handful of basket makers remained. Black ash, the material used in basketry, was rare because of disease and habitat destruction. In the early 1990s, the Council at Akwasasne began planting black ash trees in an effort to preserve them. They have now planted more than six thousand.

Mary Adams, born in 1917 to the Wolf Clan of the Mohawk, was an outstanding artist in this endangered art form. She did not receive formal education until she was sixteen. Her father was a steelworker, often gone for a long time to the city. From the time Mary was six years old, her mother taught her how to make traditional baskets. Mary married at age seventeen and raised twelve children, helping provide for them with her baskets. Finally, at age fifty, she became financially secure and was able to concentrate more on the purely artistic aspects of her craft. Her work became famous and is displayed in many museums, including the Smithsonian Institution. Her Mohawk and Catholic heritage can be seen in her work.

Soapstone, which is also known as steatite, is a metamorphic rock having a talc base. Soapstone can be recognized by its ease of carving, soapy feel, and vibrant color. Because it is easy to shape, it has been used as a carving material for centuries.

The *Pope Basket* was her greatest achievement. It was created and presented to John Paul II in 1980 to commemorate the beatification of Kateri Tekakwitha. A devout Catholic, Mary Adams wanted to do something very special to honor Kateri. She struggled with ideas for the design, but the right design finally came to her in a dream. The big bas-

Mary Adams presented an elaborate woven basket to Pope John Paul II in 1980 to commemorate the beatification of Kateri Tekakwitha.

ket she created is decorated with many tiny baskets that move when it is shaken. The shape of the basket is similar to Michelangelo's grand dome of St. Peter's Basilica. The sweet grass used in the basket's construction is sacred to the Mohawk people. During the commemoration ceremony, the Pope offered prayers for Mary Adams. His prayers helped her believe she would be lucky and continue her tradition of making baskets—and her hopes came true. During her life, she produced more than twenty-five thousand baskets.

Pottery is another ancient Haudenosaunee art form. When Europeans brought unbreakable copper pots to North America, the practical need for pottery bowls ended. For a time, the People of the Longhouse forgot how to make clay vessels. In recent years, though, the process has been rediscovered.

Clay is taken from the ground and carefully prepared by sifting and adding materials that give it more strength. The clay is then formed carefully by hand. Traditional pottery is fired outside using wood fires, while more modern-style pieces are fired in a **kiln**. Some Iroquois artists re-create the beautiful and functional work of their ancestors. They make pots with

Contemporary Iroquois artists combine ancient symbolism with modern techniques.

Tonto's Revenge *by Tom Huff makes fun of a popular hero. Harry Smith played Tonto in* The Lone Ranger *television series. Smith was a Mohawk from the Six Nations Reserve in Brantford, Ontario.*

This intricately beaded image of the Great White Pine of Peace adorns the cover of a handmade book, relating The Words That Come Before All Else. *It was made by Tom Porter.*

rounded bottoms and finely carved lines or faces on the top rim. Other Iroquois potters sculpt modern subjects, including humorous or political pieces.

Tammy Tarbell-Boehning is a modern potter who was raised near the Onondaga Indian Reservation in New York. Her Mohawk culture is vital for her life and art. She studied graphic art at Onondaga Community College and at Syracuse University, where she received a bachelor of fine arts degree. As a college student, she loved clay, and since college she has specialized in ceramics. She creates the shapes and designs of old-style Iroquois pottery and uses traditional materials such as feathers, hides, and glass beads. She also makes modern sculptures that portray today's American Indian women. In these, she tries to capture Native American women's spiritual way of life. Her work can be seen in art shows and museum collections across North America.

The Six Nations can boast that they have a great number of talented artists. These artists work in a wide variety of artistic styles. Whether re-creating ancient pottery or painting abstract acrylics on canvas, their art expresses the continuing vitality of today's Haudenosaunee people.

Tanner Bluewolf sets up his shot during practice with the Oneida Nation lacrosse clinic, summer of 2002. Lacrosse is Canada's national sport and is enjoyed by players throughout the United States and Canada.

Chapter 7

Contributions to the World

Ray Fadden speaks quickly and eloquently. This gray-haired Mohawk educator points out that the lifestyle North Americans enjoy today reflects more the lives of the first North Americans than that of the Europeans at the time of their arrival. The foods we eat—potatoes, corn, beans, cranberries, maple syrup, and so on—are gifts from Indian cultivation. Medicines that save thousands of lives today were almost all known to Native healers in long-ago times. The bouncing rubber ball and a team game that involved putting the ball through hoops are gifts from the Indians of Central America. America's democratic government, with two forms of representatives, is patterned after that of the Iroquois. The historical contributions of Native Americans are a huge part of everyday North American life today. The Iroquois also contributed one of Canada's and the United States' favorite sports—the game of *lacrosse*.

Many people think hockey is Canada's national sport, but it isn't. Lacrosse is. Queen Victoria declared lacrosse to be Canada's national sport after a traveling team of Mohawks introduced the sport to excited crowds in England. According to Iroquois tradition, lacrosse is older than the human race. The game of lacrosse can be traced all the way back to the Haudenosaunee creation story.

Just before human beings were created, Sapling and Flint, the twin sons of Sky Woman, struggled for control of the world. The first contest between them was a game of lacrosse. It was a tie, so they went on to other contests.

Lacrosse came to be a "medicine game," one of the ancient sacred healing ceremonies. Ceremonial lacrosse games are still used for healing sick persons today.

Lacrosse is also popular simply as a sport. Thousands of students, both Native and non-Indian, in high school and college play the game across

The Haudenosaunee name for lacrosse means "the Creator's game." In the old days, there could be as many as fifty players on a team, and goals would be different villages—not just goals on a field. It was a game of skill, not brutal competition.

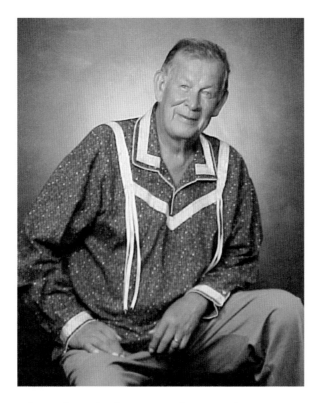

The largest producer of wooden lacrosse sticks in North America is Tuskewe Krafts, located on the Tuscarora Nation in Sanborn, New York. Tuskewe Krafts was founded by John "Wesley" Patterson Jr., a Tuscarora athlete who turned his passion for the game into a successful global business. His playing career spanned more than thirty years, as he played on the reserve, at college, and in Canada. John Patterson was inducted in the WNY/Rochester Lacrosse Hall of Fame, Springfield College Athletic Hall of Fame, Native American Sports Hall of Fame, the Ontario (Canada) Lacrosse Hall of Fame (1998), and the U.S. Lacrosse Hall of Fame (2000).

North America today. The Iroquois Nationals are the only indigenous national team competing in international sports. The team competed in the 1998 World Field Lacrosse Championships in Baltimore, Maryland. Out of eleven nations, the Iroquois took fourth place, the best showing for a national team.

Lacrosse isn't the only thing the Iroquois have contributed to the world;

Joanne Shenandoah, Wolf Clan member of the Oneida, has performed at Woodstock and the White House.

the Six Nations have produced outstanding talent in the performing arts as well. For example, Joanne Shenandoah, a Wolf Clan member of the Oneida, is an award-winning composer and singer.

Shenandoah combines traditional Haudenosaunee songs with modern "trance" instrumentals, and she is known for her outstanding voice. She has performed at the White House, she was the opening act at Woodstock '94, and she performed at President Clinton's **inauguration** and at a private performance for First Lady Hillary Clinton and Tipper Gore. Joanne Shenandoah's latest CD is titled *Peacemaker's Journey*. Sung in the Mohawk language, the album tells the story of Peacemaker's efforts to establish the Great Peace (see chapter two). Her music shows how longhouse ways continue to have a profound effect on the world today.

Robbie Robertson, yet another Iroquois musician, has been an important rock artist for almost forty years. The son of a Jewish father and

Mohawk mother, he played with Bob Dylan's world tour in 1965–1966. His group, The Band, was world famous for the next decade. He made movie sound tracks and worked with the Irish rock band U2 in the early 1980s, and in 1987, he produced his first solo recording. In 1998, with encouragement from his friends in U2, he produced *Contact from the Underworld of Red Boy*. The entire CD reflects Indian perspectives on life, combined with pow-wow drumming and hip-hop rhythms. It includes *People of the Longhouse*, a tribute to his Mohawk ancestry and Handsome Lake. Robertson also supervised the music for the movie *Gangs of New York*.

The next generation of Iroquois musical artists is coming along well. Derek Miller is Mohawk, raised on Canada's Six Nation Reservation. He has been playing blues-based rock for fourteen years, and he's compared to Neil Young, Jimmy Hendrix, and Bob Dylan. His **virtuoso** guitar **licks** and high-energy performances have won rave reviews from musicians and critics. He released an album in 2002 titled *Music Is the Medicine*.

One of the best-known Iroquois performing artists is Graham Greene,

Graham Greene, an Oneida from Six Nations Reserve in Ontario, Canada, is famous for his movie roles.

Words to the Nations

These are our times and our responsibilities. Every human being has a sacred duty to protect the welfare of our Mother Earth, from which all life comes. In order to do this, we must recognize the enemy within us. We must begin with ourselves. We must live in harmony with the natural world and recognize that excessive exploitation can only lead to our own destruction. We cannot trade the welfare of our future generations for profit now. We must abide by the Natural Law or be victim of its ultimate reality. We must stand together, the four sacred colors of man, as the one family we are in the interest of peace.

—Leon Shenandoah, Tododaho (address to the General Assembly of the United Nations)

Tom Porter, whose Mohawk name is Sakokwenionkwas, is spokesman and spiritual leader for Kanatsiohareke, a reestablished Mohawk community in New York's Mohawk Valley.

an Oneida from the Six Nations Reserve in Ontario, Canada. He is best known for playing Native American roles. His characters are always positive and dignified—but he doesn't think of himself as being political or a spokesman for Native actors. Instead, Graham Greene says he is simply an actor who tries to do a good job in all his roles. He has been in dozens of movies, but is best known for *Dances with Wolves*.

Members of the Six Nations have played significant roles in ecological, cultural, and educational realms as well. Tom Porter is the spokesman and spiritual leader of Kanatsiohareke, in New York State's Mohawk Valley. His Mohawk name is Sakokwenionkwas—"the One Who Wins." He raised his six children in the traditional way and has served in many positions on the Mohawk Nation Council of Chiefs. In the 1960s, he organized the White Roots of Peace, a group of Iroquois who toured North America encouraging Native peoples to embrace their own traditions. He helped to found the Akwesasne Freedom School, whose goal is to **revitalize** Mohawk culture, traditions, and language. Porter also worked at Partridge House, a drug and alcohol rehabilitation center at Akwesasne. In 1993, Tom Porter and a small group of traditional Mohawk people reestablished Kanatsiohareke in the homeland of the Mohawk people as a place promoting the revitalization of Mohawk ways. He serves as the Native American chaplain for Native inmates in the New York State prison system.

Jake Swamp is another individual who has had a significant impact on preserving Iroquois ways and spreading the Great Peace to other nations. He is Wolf Clan subchief of the Mohawk, representing them at the Grand Council. He founded the Tree of Peace Society, whose goal is to educate people about Haudenosaunee culture, peace, and the environment. During the Clinton administration, Jake Swamp met with the president to discuss Native and ecological issues. Swamp has also addressed the United Nations. He teaches at ten universities each year and has written a number of books. Because of his efforts, environmentalists, peace activists, and other Native communities have been enriched by the traditions of the Haudenosaunee.

Like Swamp, Ray Fadden has done much, both for his people and for all of North America. In his book *Iroquois Culture and Commentary*, Doug George-Kanentiio describes Ray Fadden as a "Miracle Man" and "revolutionary." Born in 1910, Fadden's bloodline is largely Scottish—but his wife is Mohawk, and he was adopted into the Wolf Clan. He graduated from Fredonia Normal School. After earning his teaching degree from State

Ray Fadden's teaching encouraged American Indians to realize how much they have contributed to the world.

University of New York in Plattsburgh, Fadden taught school at Akwesasne and Onchiota. At the time, schools still communicated the idea that Indians were "ignorant savages." Ray did extensive research, rediscovering the great role First Nations people had in the creation of today's American culture. He also established the Six Nations Museum, which can be visited in Onchiota, New York.

Ray Fadden is one of those special teachers who combines an amazing depth of knowledge with an emotional, hard-hitting style of presentation. His teaching has had an incredible impact on the Iroquois leadership of today: Jake Swamp, Tom Porter, and Julius Cook were all his students.

His impact has spread beyond the Six Nations as well. As George-Kanentiio explains: "It is no exaggeration to say Ray Fadden's innovative teaching methods and grasp of history have been responsible for a new wave of scholarship in America, one which has finally begun to treat Natives as fully functioning human beings who have contributed greatly to the world."

Iroquois athletes, singers, actors, activists, and teachers are as active and effective today as they have been at any time in history. They inspire their own nations—and the larger North American society as well. The Haudenosaunee today continue to enrich all of our lives.

Powwows are social and cultural, but not sacred events. Members of the Six Nations, along with Indians from all over the United States and Canada, participate in these celebrations.

Chapter 8

Challenges for Today, Hopes for the Future

Brian Patterson remembers the tragic events that began Turning Stone Casino—and he is well pleased with the way it has worked out for the Oneida tribe today.

Back in the 1980s the Oneida only held 32 acres (13 hectares) of land. Reservation life trapped people in a vicious cycle of poverty. There were problems with teen suicide, dropping out of school, and alcoholism. Most tribal members lived in substandard trailers, which were firetraps. In one fire, two Oneida people lost their lives—the local fire department, located off the reservation, did not respond. Ray Halbritter, who was chief at the time, firmly resolved that his people would become economically self-sufficient, whatever it took.

Turning Stone Casino turned the tide of poverty and helplessness for the Oneida. Along with the casino, the Oneida have an 800-seat Las Vegas-style showroom, which shows some of the most popular acts in the country. There are also nine restaurants, a 258-room hotel, and a 175-site RV park. Money from the casino has allowed the tribe to buy back large

The Oneida Nation contributed $10 million to assist in the building of the new National Museum of the American Indian in Washington, D.C.

amounts of tribal land. As a result of casino funds, the Oneida have guaranteed scholarships for academically successful Oneida students. They have also created an early learning center for children, a work-learn program for teens, and an elder care facility. The unsafe trailers have been replaced by neat, new homes for all residents of the reservation. A new health center provides state-of-the-art medical care. Oneida Textile Designs, a talent agency called Skydancer Television Productions, and a host of other businesses have spun off from the casino. Topping it all off, the Oneidas have become the first Indian nation in America to send back their share of federal Indian money. And they were still able to donate $10 million to the Smithsonian Institution to help build its new National Museum of the American Indian.

What used to be called gambling is now called gaming. It has also been called "the new buffalo." Like the bison, money from gaming is now providing all the necessities of life for some Indians. Ernie Stevens, Oneida, is chairperson of National Indian Gaming Association. He says: "Who would have imagined the great opportunities that gaming would have brought us? It makes me proud to see reservations that were once depressed and impoverished become the thriving communities that they are today. We can only go up from here."

Indian gaming has undeniably brought economic aid to the Oneida, but it has also been criticized. Handsome Lake's code warns against gambling: it can become addictive and "cause hardship in families by depriving them of their basic needs." Doug George-Kanentiio has written an editorial titled, "Why Traditional Iroquois Are Opposed to Gambling Casinos":

> The Haudenosaunee have fought long and hard against commercial gambling. This struggle between the pro- and anti-gambling elements in our communities has resulted in violence leading to the death of several Iroquois. The Confederacy has repeatedly condemned gambling as an endeavor that exploits the human spirit while leading to greed and corruption.

The people of the Six Nations will probably not agree on this issue for a long time to come. In the meantime, all Iroquois agree that yet another challenge must be faced—the possible loss of their languages.

Gaming has been called the "new buffalo," since it holds the promise of providing many needs for North American Indian communities. Less than twenty-four Indian casinos have been successful enough to substantially impact their nations. Turning Stone Casino, of the Oneida Nation, is one of these.

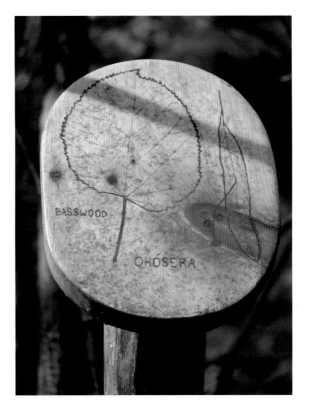

Kanatsiohareke is committed to the revitalization of the Mohawk language. Labels in the woods there are in English and Mohawk.

A 1996 survey found that 10 percent of Mohawks speak their language; the other Iroquois nations found even smaller percentages. Loss of language is a serious problem, since according to many experts, 50 percent of a culture's identity is tied to language. Loss of tribal language also means the loss of esteem, identity, and the ability to defend against *exploitation* by non-Indians.

Many programs are working to revitalize Iroquois languages. The Akwesasne Freedom School, for example, is a school where students speak and learn in Mohawk. The school stresses the role of family in teaching language and culture. Parents are encouraged to speak Mohawk at home and to learn their language if they don't know it. The school not only teaches the Mohawk language, it communicates a whole Mohawk worldview. The curriculum is based on the Words that Come Before All Else (see chapter three). Students learn how to care for Mother Earth. Recently, pupils at the Freedom School planted three thousand trees to create a forest. They also learned how to make baskets from black ash and how to tap maple trees to produce syrup.

Kanatsiohareke (pronounced "ga-na-jo-ha-lay-gay") is a special place of hope for the Mohawk people. Two hundred years ago, the Mohawk were driven from their beautiful land in the Mohawk Valley. A prophecy was made then that they would someday return. In the summer of 1993, that vision was fulfilled, due largely to the efforts of Tom Porter. Three hundred and twenty-two acres (130 hectares) of riverfront land was obtained at auction. When the Mohawks moved onto the property, nearby townspeople placed a large sign on the barn: "WELCOME HOME."

Sunflowers like those grown at Kanatsiohareke are just one of the earth's bountiful gifts. Many Iroquois look to the future while maintaining their ancestors' close connection to the earth.

Kanatsiohareke means "the place of the clean pot." It is the original name of that region, referring to large kettle holes in a nearby stream that form swirling eddies of water. It is also a metaphor for a place where minds—and hearts—can be renewed. Kanatsiohareke is a place for spiritual healing for many people. Native and non-Native alike have felt at home there.

One of the many projects at Kanatsiohareke is Mohawk *language immersion*. For the last five summers, classes have been offered for children and adults, from beginning to advanced level, in the Mohawk language. Many students take the opportunity to study their language at Kanatsiohareke, even though it means time away from family, community, and jobs. Kanatsiohareke provides a unique opportunity for students to learn their language and culture within the homeland of their ancestors.

The community runs a bed-and-breakfast where both Natives and non-Natives can stay. There is an arts and crafts store, which sells examples of traditional and contemporary work made by Indians from North and South America. This store is an outstanding source of books and tapes teaching about Native American history, art, traditions, culture, and language.

At the beginning of a new millenium, the People of the Longhouse are a diverse group. Members of the Six Nations can be found on the busy streets of Brooklyn . . . and in the deep woods of the Canadian North. Some devote their lives to the Christian faith; many follow the way of Handsome Lake. Some work in the high-tech offices of modern casinos; others farm the soil.

Their challenge is to keep their ancient unity as a people while meeting the demands of the twenty-first century. As they meet this challenge, they will continue to contribute to the larger society. Like their forefathers, the Iroquois today enrich the lives of those around them.

Further Reading

George-Kanentiio, Doug. *Iroquois Culture and Commentary*. Santa Fe, N.M.: Clear Light Publishers, 2000.

Mitchell, Mike (Kanentakeron). *Traditional Teachings*. Cornwall Island, Ont.: North American Indian Travelling College, 1984.

Swamp, Jake. *Giving Thanks: A Native American Good Morning Message*. New York: Lee & Low Books, 1995.

Tehanetorens (Ray Fadden). *Legends of the Iroquois*. Santa Fe, N.M.: Clear Light Publishers, 1998.

Wallace, Paul. *White Roots of Peace: The Iroquois Book of Life*. Santa Fe, N.M.: Clear Light Publishers, 1998.

Weatherford, Jack. *Native Roots: How the Indians Enriched America*. New York: Fawcett Columbine, 1991.

For More Information

Haudenosaunee Home Page
www.sixnations.org

The Mohawk Valley Project—Kanatsiohareke
www.design-site.net/mohawk.htm

Oneida Indian Nation Homepage
oneida-nation.net/

Peace 4 Turtle Island
www.peace4turtleisland.org

The Wampum Chronicles
www.wampumchronicles.com

Publisher's Note:

The Web sites listed on this page were active at the time of publication. The publisher is not responsible for Web sites that have changed their address or discontinued operation since the date of publication. The publisher will review and update the Web sites upon each reprint.

Glossary

abrogate: To abolish or treat as nonexistent.

artifacts: Something created by humans for practical use.

beatified: Declared to have a blessedness. Beatification is a step to being declared a saint.

clan: A clan is a group of families who are descended from a common ancestor.

confederacy: A group formed for a common purpose.

consolation: The state of being comforted, often from great sorrow.

constitution: The basic principles and laws of a nation.

criteria: A set of standards upon which a decision or judgment is made.

decimate: To reduce drastically, often in a destructive way.

dictators: A person who rules with complete control.

diverse: Differing from each other.

domestic: Relating or originating to one's own country.

economic: Relating to the production, distribution, and use of goods and services.

executive: Someone with administrative or managerial responsibilities.

exploitation: An act of using someone or something unjustly for one's own benefit.

feminism: The theory of the political, economic, and social equality of the sexes.

Great Depression: The period of low economic activity and rising levels of unemployment that began in 1929 lasting until 1939.

inauguration: A ceremony marking a beginning, such as the installation of a new president.

inclusive: Covering all items, services, or people.

indigenous: Something that occurs naturally in an area.

instigated: Urged forward, made happen.

kiln: An oven capable of reaching extremely high temperatures that is used to bake (fire) pottery.

lacrosse: A game in which players use long sticks with a pouch on the end to catch, carry, and toss a ball, with the purpose of throwing the ball into the opposing team's goal.

language immersion: A method of learning a language in which only the language being taught is used.

licks: Musical flourishes.

medicine woman: A priestly healer.

memory device: Something used to trigger a memory.

migrated: Moved from one place to another.

post-traumatic stress disorder: A psychological disorder caused by a highly stressful event.

representation: The action of one person standing for the interests of another.

repatriation: When governments or individuals return to Indian nations the sacred remains of Native ancestors or religious and artistic treasures that belong with the Indian nation who made them.

revered: Adored, held in high esteem.

revitalize: To give new life to.

sexism: Behaviors or attitudes that foster stereotypes of social roles based on gender.

smallpox: A contagious disease characterized by skin eruptions and scarring.

smudge pot: A container holding a smoldering mass that is used in an attempt to prevent damage from frost.

subvert: To corrupt by an undermining of morals or faith.

suffrage: The right to vote.

suppress: To put down.

traditionalists: Those who continue to practice the beliefs and customs they inherited from their own cultures rather than from other cultures.

trusteeship: Supervisory control of a group or country.

virtuoso: Someone who excels in one of the arts.

Western: Relating to the culture of Europe and America.

white sage: An herb used in ceremonies and healing.

Index

Biographies

Kenneth McIntosh is a pastor, and his wife Marsha is a schoolteacher. They both took leave from their regular jobs to work on this series. Formerly, Kenneth worked as a junior high teacher in Los Angeles, California. He wrote *Clergy* for the Mason Crest series "Careers with Character." The McIntoshes live in upstate New York and have two children, Jonathan and Eirené. They are grateful for the opportunity this work has given them to travel and meet with many wonderful Native people.

Martha McCollough received her bachelor's and master's degrees in anthropology at the University of Alaska-Fairbanks, and she now teaches at the University of Nebraska. Her areas of study are contemporary Native American issues, ethnohistory, and the political and economic issues that surround encounters between North American Indians and Euroamericans.

Benjamin Stewart, a graduate of Alfred University, is a freelance photographer and graphic artist. He traveled across North America to take the photographs included in this series.